So What So That

Also by Marjorie Welish

The Annotated "Here" and Selected Poems
In the Futurity Lounge / Asylum for Indeterminacy
Isle of the Signatories
Word Group

Coffee House Press   Minneapolis   2016

So what So that

POEMS

MARJORIE WELISH

Coffee House Press books are available to the trade through our primary distributor, Consortium Book Sales & Distribution, cbsd .com or (800) 283-3572. For personal orders, catalogs, or other information, write to info@coffeehousepress.org.

Coffee House Press is a nonprofit literary publishing house. Support from private foundations, corporate giving programs, government programs, and generous individuals helps make the publication of our books possible. We gratefully acknowledge their support in detail in the back of this book.

LIBRARY OF CONGRESS CATALOGING-IN-PUBLICATION DATA

Names: Welish, Marjorie, 1944-, author.
Title: So what so that : poems / Marjorie Welish.
Description: Minneapolis : Coffee House Press, 2016.
Identifiers: LCCN 2016016172 | ISBN 9781566894562 (paperback)
Subjects: | BISAC: POETRY / American / General.
Classification: LCC PS3573.E4565 A6 2016 | DDC 811/.54—dc23
LC record available at https://lccn.loc.gov/2016016172

PRINTED IN THE UNITED STATES OF AMERICA

23 22 21 20 19 18 17 16   1 2 3 4 5 6 7 8

Acknowledgments

Some poems in this volume have appeared previously:

Birmingham Poetry Review: "Cardiac"

Chicago Review: "from Of Autobiography"

Conjunctions: "Folding Cythera," "Prospects Of and At"

Fence: "Song of the Three"

The Harvard Advocate: "Expulsion: A Walking Tour"

Lana Turner: "Griot Riot," "Left-Handed," "So What," "Vamp ('Avant-pied')"

OR: "When He's the Most Interesting"

VLAK: "As Technique / As Device /," "An Ordinary Evening Plus or Minus"

Best American Experimental Writing (Omnidawn, 2014): "Fray"

Some Pigeons Are More Equal Than Others (Lars Müller Publishing, 2015): "Sayings"

The author gratefully acknowledges the John Simon Guggenheim Memorial Foundation for supporting the completion of *So What So That.*

Contents

I.

II.

So What So That

Part I.

So That: So What

So What

          And from

As if   as if

Yet it   of a

But be   the text

If it   out by

Of an   those in

Be that   such that

Let not   what so

As to   it as

With his   but not

To beg   of that

It on   or at

One hand   whereas

So that   so what

Goes off   no iffs

Left-Handed

Epistrophy   fundamental
Hums   it was a nasal syringe
Undulating forthwith   liquid
Of small assemblies yes   reedy
Aperture wreckage re-released
Neat anapest   changing does change
Silhouette   negative jump up
Stethoscope no chaser   else breaks
A fundamental Picasso
A double fundamental half
False start   half body and
Water running   minor seventh
Tenement denunciations
Three accents to every protest

You Needn't

Irritability   a word
Has words with   may I have a war
Constituted   of alternative takes.
Whereupon an accident   is to say
Or sting letting things down   where did you put
the unconditional love   take this take
uninterruptedly an ear
tapped flat   with a tincture of hit or miss.
Move and be moved   is misheard verbatim.
The bent sound played   on the ride cymbal in
ticklish oncoming traffic   what's this? A stringed
instrument with   a prominent forehead
taking the brunt of a word.   Probably
the word for *Go*! The word *Up*!   A comma.

For a few odes not found on the native scale
Hereafter a mumble in upheaval   ploughshares
May have words may I make pronunciations   much
and dusted in rehearsal. Letting things fall also
unattended a minute   an ear's common
furrow as brushed by moths   moths' pity and beating
brushes are specialists   very characteristic
beating of wings or nothing   what's this iota

of oncoming traffic and where   did you mishear
verbatim? What's the probability you did
satisfy the said accident with cicadas
and a smattering of swords, an earful.
A stringed instrument with an early-warning system
alternative takes   taking the brunt of bespoke.

When He's the Most Interesting

When he is most at rest when he is mostly a surface
When he is utmost slaughter commemorative
When most self or a much much improved antihistamine
When he is infinitesimal infinitesimal information
Most costly intercom Klangfarben and the ever-lovely Glenn Branca
hideous to normal aging but not to quarrel withdrawal improvising
trouble a last-minute substitute beset opaque and local bandwidth
from cities a crash course in octaves a lot of in this inhaling:
"to induce or persuade to participate or engage"
"to be between to make a difference"
"right title legal share in something" breath taking
"participation in advantage and responsibility"
"a charge for borrowed money usually a percentage"
"an excess above what is due"

Most interesting from under a valve cracked a surge or Klangfarben
is a studio cooled from above the art subject to
impairment in the speech of the ever-lovely lawn sprinkler
for a costly mist's rewriting the interior mostly as surface—
an incentive to change one's mind: "to be between to make a
    difference"
"an excess above what is due" instrumentally conceived
does some husky support "right title the legal share"
quavers "usually a percentage" "of advantage and responsibility"

herewith enclosed much much textual hassle utmost almost mostly
streams hurry a surface in octaves palms disruptive immediately
after this at most commemorative however you may be beset
assailed by ornaments information harassed by appearances
rest at a premium when he is received nearest the torrent
and devoted allotment of wall and floor, "the level base of a room."

And so very far and away the ever-lovely surge
herewith enclosed much much textual hassle utmost almost mostly
quavers "usually a percentage" "of advantage and responsibility"
studio cooled from above the art is subject to
change one's mind "to be between to make a difference"
after this at most commemorative however you may be beset
cluttered disenfranchised harassed by itinerant appearances
"an excess above what is due" instrumentally conceived
excess except excessive exceedingly exchanged
exceptionally husky does some "right title legal share"
at a premium when he is most near the door
with an allotment of wall and floor "the level base of a room."
When he is most interesting he is nettlesome wreckage
promised you promised effluence effluent effluvium efflux

Vocalese

. . . walked off disinterested in opinion   interested in mappa mundi

throws some shade   at high noon hour before dawn exited from post hoc propter hoc scat   that

A dip in opinion a decline in they who berate them these   notes a dip in the crash course they went offline to happen take the plunge in sounds sounding out declivities   Why Not streaming live

And even an unpitched splice in the enigma for which no dilatory dearth can adequately express the exit composed in advance

Now or Never music to some audience noise degree zero do disenchant   eyes ears nose and throat to the barricades' surplus and lack   have not slept in circuit   anything but dim perplexity   utility in whose rhetoric is Mind Your Business

during the solo throughout the course of resilience   intermittently as is   battered a severe region with accidents which when taken up are intentions' freeze so much so then   we lived together in a changed plot

Baring the device the hero walked off the   occupant walked off the stage and into a state of affairs   to rehearse this alarm   freeze frame does not fit   specialists therein eclipse you   out of work and into work peopled a duo   a quartet might so imagine its experimental hydraulics

to an idea   thought plan mental representation about beginning
the incident that initiates   certifies dispatch

after the solo   through the oval into the cistern brochures antici-
pated the election amped each catch basin   each amazed catch
evaluating the curb for remote overtones   nonpareil D Dorian

And coming toward us: passenger submerged in his seat bystander
drawn from the stereotype public-at-large a congregation

Our sonorous causes crossed in the post. I have been rereading
your letters, constant companion. I have been reassembling your
remembered words, arena. Constant companion to hero a schema
may at times gut the stage. Under the eaves our modal hero turned
his back on catcalls   charivari from

character + bound motif exited   central consciousness walked
off the stage   elected to go   elected ethos to retire the staircase
provided   left the slipcase   sauntered off strode away

To obey / not obey oral / written cadenza in memory   rehearse
spontaneity in motto that cuts coinage of self nonexistent for a
sec   in gratitude eventful   federation of singularities at Weimar
informing the everywhere through the gate qualitative   and in
close selves whereby sundry essays were to attract academies that
would confer poetry on the votive offering

beyond the pale

He shredded the frame   he punctured the screen the space of *the
the*   stage ebbed   the space reaped a rehearsal rescued a helpful

infill for what it's worth recalibrated partition   between live and
life he gives a lift to the supplement   supple supplement hurried
off hearsay say so bestowed a kind of suspended sentence that the
other might not yet hear you when the fire engine interrupts your
thoughts   and mien which then continue once the screaming is
over   if so what by music enough we throw flatted fifths into the
kiln   for salt   glaze redoubt glyph   emplacement   sizable
earthworks sent   common cause indifferent to its own fate
wound salt in the glyph incision thrown   salt in the scriptorium
disinterested in small talk lights gels yet in what goes on

hour before dawn   octave not talking

Cardiac

Come heart-aches

Bitter breast-care

reap aches bitterly bin carefully bitten care hear weight weights
    weighted breast your weight you are heavily upon me you have
    taken all space and time come heart whose arch you acquire

    at half-mast
the four-color

intellect

    Forethought

I like you but would like you better without this weight upon me
    you usurp all of me you employer of help of my heart at the helm
    of my heart

    enervating scrap
scraped another just weight a just weight

to translate flight all of it on shoulders the thesaurus treasury care to
    breast dour roving undertaken by others heed loose change

dear to harrow

      hello compounded

with probable epilogue and lures and who knows knots enabling
    another reader seaworthy the full story more if only to change
    our reading of the red yellow blue we knew

      gloves to engulf
coloring self from rival expulsion

let me do all the waiting as those posts dwell to contour a heart bin
    in the wind of acedia wherein much existence many essays

      so that:

discontent

      something like *poor paste*

      and chance

Granular Polyvocality

> *At the beginning of a transformation towards*
> *asymmetry, exceptional events. . . .*
> IANNIS XENAKIS

I

In a rowboat timing that lightning

the timing that lightning versifies

versifies *the timing of thunder desperate and harried,* she sd.

In a tent a man is timing frequencies of high-fidelity storms

available for

method later.

Flutter

guide and tirade

of his, she sd, with rights and privileges

the volleys and wire entanglements

speaking maximally ad hoc;

probabilistic goes

the harvested leap

into pavilion.

[. . .] *the enrichment and the leap*

the external conflicts

reap all, some, nonexistent fish

counting the frequencies.

The tent ripples.

Flutter

may be aflame.

Skittishness in between filaments, as translation is.

WZBC *desperate and harried*
sd of he who
rubbed overt cantos
with backtalk loitering amid tetrachords;
as though lost

he hauls several short storms
to the dais.
To the ear
a montage of polyvocality

adjusted for ballast and interest throughout how many flagrant
    microphones
in dulcet barrage and vocal megaphones to the lost choral
    seriousness
and she: "I thought the inadequacy of the object to the idea

was the point." They all stop speaking
verbatim sentences unabridged din and outages to the idea.

A far orator
sets one microphone farther
fetched from the scar
to the ear.

2
I. X. in a tent
in a text A ZBC
M. W. in a test

Of the ear in sea-surge
rehearsing a rare event:
the voice
of many

acoustically adjusted to compensate for vocally unequal
reap as that which came to the throat *stochastically.*
Unrivalled moment therefore and until
after much, someone new enters and, reaching

to reposition the mic
to compensate

for the placement
he saw as bane
not what he would have heard
as bane, undid sound
balance unequivocally.

Desperate and harried cloud
loitering backtalk amid tetrachords
the many speaking simultaneously:
a vocal glut glissandi insisted
shout-out to rehearsal put the viscous
microphone distant a few inches
away, distinctly

elastic shout-out to testing supposition,
deposits the microphone farther
to compensate; last minute
next minute reset upset by one,
who, crossing the podium
in no time reaps that out-of-alignment
prior acoustic.

Test text tempest reset
upset set interest polyp
polyptych to the air

to the ear rarely heard:
you could write with it.

Set upset polymath to the ear
resize the point they all spoke
text tent to the air crash course in
the one many agitprop pent up
in the upset ear: we heard

all alignment acoustic ballast
for the many pent-up narratives'
yearlings apparatus
through self-proclaimed polyptych.
You could write with it.

3

Voice the voicing collective reflecting on the effect of hearing itself
    fallible
abrasive prodigal sentences half again as much yes, but one more
    forceful
in public extraordinary peppercorn so the handicap; thus the
    anomaly to the eye.
Iotas saturating the ornate heat with shout-out as they, preparing fray,
assemble, replete earshot rooster allotted some distant position
in the ensemble. Now rehearsing: the famished furnace.

Now rehearsing the famished furnace, delectable

shouts a crash course they all stopped speaking

amid microphones dedicated to steep equality:

more than enough table thought the inadequacy

on point, even the din sets one microphone farther

from the mouth of the big man.

Farther from the mouth the microphone in loitering half again

starved famished prolix acoustically copious sentences saturating
the heat

with storming tendencies adequate to the here and now rehearsing
takes except

where deregulated in loitering melodic pumps—let's make the
collective

Be Somebody. Accordion foldout. In preparing fray for nonet, the
technician

dealt with the microphone.

4

Throughout electrical malfunctioning, she sd,

is loss of tone

as though a tonal ought: *too strident*

Debit or credit?

A man fishes from a boat.

He is endeavoring to fold
a stormy microphone the spokes of
orchestras also in folk

far-fetched ear compensated.

Harvested glissandi
the valid fish reach reap
electrostatic discharge within
massively so pent up

contra and ariel

that then do inform
eclectic whispers seen:
accident from affect, accidental affidavit, you
in the dinghy . . .

And hell without dignity.

Song of the Three

1

I really enjoy time's arrow.
"If you find a new metaphor . . . ,"
he floated a prompt vertigo

under his breath.

2

Eternity, first alone; *logic, so of no use.*
A guide to the merest
provision, brushstrokes went forth.

Hello, the destroyer.

. . . gentle slopes broken by earth-works
with crashing densities near the surface
entice us to cut there, silver

then insolvency
then maxims for warmth.

3

Then comes plenty

from *a man who does not want to hear*

scarcity

notwithstanding the near behemoth

from which culture emerges

exaggerated.

But not only this.

And a day attended us

as we seized the lever,

the elevator, the grammar of plot

for our redoubt:

to inveigh against

the literature, *with air on the road*

handed to do, to obey, not to do, not to obey—

all with horses.

Alive to

mutabilites on horseback

is the portable diadem

the coiled spring

which is memory.

O body and soul

scrivening
indices to read a checklist
against which throbs the aperçu

of symptom

trying for a good night's hilarity.
O why! *O why light-bound and bent in!*

And from an eye *they pulled the sphere
into a cylinder.*

Prospects Of and At

I

Caesura hath me a chisel
Greater growth isn't

A stay. Accelerate
Georgics. Park etc.

Caesura made me
Stop. A sort of scramble

Greater caesura
Abruptly a ha-ha

Resolves what is isn't
A house the how of

Rasps in our lives
Sounding boards.

Call particles'
Greater growth.

Too close to the speaker
Speakers should be forward

Of the piano.

A stick accelerates stickiness
        selectively is selectively adhesive.
And his rustics were wanting.

Wrong end of the stick tempted us.

Eyes on gray
        Gray scale eyes grayness become verge
As wet eyes locate the heart
        as wet eyes locate the heart's wetlands:

slate graphite pewter steel locale.

Relapse
        Relapse to one's inextinguishable simile
as it flails the air.

There: done.

The which way
        which lisp at the behest of caesura
on the path of the same name as that gray matter.

A lisp of divergence:

      which way to the eyesore?

Having not distraught

      metrical modulation nor his family's temperament

is *fort-da* advancing on your spill *spiel.*

Caesura fecit
Greater growth isn't

Gorgeous caesura and star
To navigate all that green grown ambient

spot didn't cup
disequilibria nor the moon

consume man for nothing
At their throats bruised arias better this time: cut.

Growth of stay caesura and breathing for stamina
Stay with me you said always sometimes

dishevelment voicing the decision: cut to
voice the late great threadbare carpet in her

vocal mastery struck much rustle. Uncut
from popular hormones above and everywhere

feral bimbos unshadowed an intestinal area
forward of the stage. Whereupon street fairs.

To avoid it step into it
        Repeat.
Avail yourself of cause and effect.
        And trouble. Whereas
revision awaits adage. (Advantage: Pound.)

By-path. The forward edge.

Caesura made me
Greater growth isn't

Emergent crayon made me
Read this. If you can read this

growth groan the groaning crayon
that verve conveys in turbulent winds.

Saturated Saturday read this. If you can read this green market
a test of spacing in a sense a pith greater than one

fish. Read this caesura in a sea of green
greenery anyway for a greater green discordant climate.

Harvested brother if you can read this
language high-yield capture of selvage salvage some eros

too deep for tears detours to occur
in between epitome and premonition

you who lovingly mistook the crow's foot
path to a distant rusticated sky and repose . . .

2
Greater caesura
Fast stare

Greater chisel made a
Resolve what is isn't

Scrambled speaking
Undergrowth and rank elegy

Emitting from the piano
As struck struck and pedaled

Technique is as close as what is isn't
Kale bok choy arugula spinach

Readies. Stops. Tone color
In an accent how growth

Stubble in flight accelerates a
Difficulty pretty much

Rasp in a scrabble
Or a dry cough

For the inner ear.
Meanwhile he is writing.

In a profuse suspense
         Is glut surfeit plethora
Lawn: cease and desist carpeting.

A change from action to rest.

Greater growth isn't
        Excess redundance
Under the rubric.

. . . the phonetic content silently to ourselves.

Medicinal botanics act face up
        At no cost unconditional and sheer
Becoming world without end.

Ready, steady, go!

Perfume to violet liaisons or violence in full dress
        Plumes smoke flounces wayfaring
Horizon. Pours. Soaks. Floods.

The study of.

Greater caesura
Rehabilitated

From the rubble
of a metropolis

stimulants

reboot facades

the likeness after

irruption in rebuilt use.

Do you remember the iconoclastic

procession from the church in halts

sampled from faces of possessed folk

apostolic unwittingly brightening and darkening?

So That + Curricula at High Noon

I

At the ready readies

weeklies bequeath said feverish

sayings

spent

flavor of the syllabus

free to move about from frequency

to wavelength for which this ice is

pro and con scarce rare very

succulent concept

Black turf black turf

worthy and somnolent:

door mat, want?

What tomorrow

lived lividly *one day at a time*

milk below

cries and the

tests they designate

at a snail's pace.

Good governance once
was to issue in a willing
relic so sayeth legacy.

Needle
know thyself
pending roots.

Pens, pens, pens
rewind snowy
rope of onions to cleave

what everyone knows
to sweep
time and tide alive alive-o

years before that
encrypted sixes and
interesting dice

diagnostics
for the liberal
tragic flaw to hail

everything of them

find everything worth

yards and ells

had to do with

thieves cant

mark the razor

buy a dialogue

  incarnate with what it means

to look for

  wind at my back.

2

So that said: read the letters

I can only say at present sayeth breaks

years before that tomorrow

lived lividly *one day at a time*

at the ready readies

weeklies bequeath said feverish

sayings come out of a clinch break

wants to know how know-how in the breaks

buried somewhere borrowed blue

said periodically
"Can I interest you in *The Big Issue*
Please don't all rush me at once"

was like fish breaking
a surface said to have the last laugh
at cracks push comes to shove in a willing
relic so sayeth legacy a sentence how to fix how to ruin
governance once break down fade throng
upon a time stymied he sd latter-day
in a manner of speaking panoramically of a prior
crossroads: apples and oranges
to look for
voluminous metropolis then these boxes

Baskets sayeth bitten Kyrie
and beaks forced to flee sleeping quarters
breaking news assaulted our mend
So that said, read the letters
I can only say at present
sayeth breaks headfirst breaking pith
sayeth breaks rush *years before that*
future perfect sayings in the clutch eggs at straws
pursuant to lamentations at hand arable
time and tide alive alive-o

fishmonger just cause of yesteryear

thinking of a number to die for

breaking stride

I can only say at present sayeth breaks

years before that morrow

lived lividly *one day at a time*

at the ready readies immediate

instanter weeklies bequeath said feverish

open source

Black turf black turf

rope of onions keep in touch

where dramatic action let

person being disobedient disturb habitat

in making letters break the surface of the unlovely tomb

credence or shelf or niche to have reference to

archaic / primitive framing differing ledgers

in order of appearance spent

flavor of the syllabus

its craft infra-thin clash

enrapt its name to hallow it

in alphabetical order free to move about subtitles

Whatever the authorities

the strand said: ask a needle and a needle and a

needle box do not forsake me

for the rain it raineth *I can only say at present*

sayeth breaks rush *years before that* future

jurisprudence going going gone struggling with

old clothes so called unexpected

break to eke out estrange from vacate

the habit of insight the habitus of flaw in awe of

breakage finds everything interestingly

know-how buried where fish knife sayeth

tines whose labor laboring to prod

matter mortar forager rusticated

breaks—yes! Ps and Qs sampling fairest

plot came then all senses so knotted

through ideology and its terror

Breaks sayeth not all has been

plummeted

3

So that said

feathery *at present*

sayeth breaks, tomorrow the eye

bequeaths said feverish iridescence *break* blackening

know-how in the embers flying back

against snowy mountains.

So that said
Read the letters
years before that, tomorrow
lived lividly one day
at the ready readies
come out of a clinch break
circuit breaker: disconnect all appliances
rewiring from the central office
will take two to three days.

Said infill
assists *the letters* colloquially
I can only say at present perpendicular to
Olympian wrists rotating writs on your mark
Sayeth breaks skimming stones
bending the *years before that, tomorrow* double
on the run *lived lividly one day at a time* as the racket swung back
at the ready readies until all have been none
by not stepping fretfully at loss accelerating coin toss on
syncopation the pavement catching and throwing the boundary
and covering one's eyes dug one bounce only
rung attempt to climb the said stick in deep.
A kind of conglomerate.

At the ready
on a table may be temporarily
stowed: in use, or overflow: which?

To the devoted page goes uncut
manufactures' bespoke adjacent
edge. Where were we?

Do you want carrot greens
broken off, says what
about produce's combustible postulates?

So that said
Read the letters
I can only say at present
sayeth breaks branching
years before that tomorrow
lived lividly one day at a time
at the ready readies
know thyself

Sun up sun down
the sign of an owl

of three minds.

So that: said precedent *read the*

    settlement's furtive penumbra of doubt

as meant the narrative magnet: intensest

    keys dangling from the quest as though he were rid of

careening decibels unenforceable but that to be writ

    cannot be amicably reversed by any power: threat

furthers heat conflict complaint filed with intrinsic adult

    dent that of a wound and iff . . . then legally;

a blow to the discursive wide road susceptible to

    grammar for incorrect sentences

wants the ammunition of the utterer nails nonredundant

    breakage in theory sensitive to indices

lived lividly: the semantic core of author.

I can only say at present

Sayeth propositions descended not sweet on expressions working up
    a sweat and semiotics for this validity

throughout breakage we get to be. Ruddy junk shall inherit the
    earth, and damages may

sayeth that at equinox the split has never scanted

propositions *at the ready readies weeklies bequeath said feverish*
    antinomies meant,

and that, if split the difference reversed epic-like transactions
    alive / dead

to affirm survival of will, then the matrix of the gift also.

Tomorrow lived lividly *one day* now or never

at the ready readies on your mark

weeklies bequeath said feverish rush

faster is better upon a star

in the breaks breach speech practices

as progressive gas: are you ready for this grease lightning?

I do not know which to prefer

said breaks

or

sayeth breaks

              spoke she

one time indivisible:

at the ready readies

              matching chairs to attendees,

or at thoroughly infinitesimal

bespoke maths

              begetting treasure for any.

It is winter *sayeth breath* with its beak
axiomatically, that is, straight across from point to point.
Saying sayings saying circles.

4
Feuilletons in grace are you ready for this

quantum leap six feet under miniscule fathom to the ear
epiphany felt it

at risk
in the law of whole-cloth names each

pebble saved by the bell like father a stone forevermore

ups and downs on a scale of one twist thick and fast sixes its mass
grease lightning *Larousse*

speech practices
drop

the fine art of a still small voice starry sky above
realia

To cause to separate

To cause to separate
uses thereof, loving

breakage:

To cause to separate
uses thereof, loving
breakage:

let no man put asunder

in war asunder the

crack in her voice

Shatter, smash, crack, snap, fracture, fragment, splinter, fall to bits,
    fall to pieces;
split, burst; fracture, crack, pierce, puncture, penetrate, perforate;
    more
cut;
decipher, decode, decrypt, unravel, work out; more
informal figure out, crack; interrupt, disturb, interfere with. "She's
    so fine."
Stop, pause, have a rest, recess; cushion, soften the impact of;

give up, relinquish, drop; more

informal kick, shake, quit, "She's so fine."

Exceed, surpass, beat, better, cap, top, outdo, outstrip, eclipse; more

contravene, violate, fail to observe, fail to comply with, infringe,
    breach; more

defy, flout, disobey, fly in the face of;

give way, crack, cave in, yield,

destroy, crush, quash, defeat, vanquish, overcome, overpower,
    overwhelm, suppress, cripple; more weaken, subdue, cow,
    undermine; change, alter, shift; more

"She's so fine."

Morning has broken magenta

Less berateage by what language, Hamlet?

How may one thwart the averages?

How may one thwart the desires of others to know your motives?

ASSIGNMENT: Through dialogue draft a scene in which the tension lies
in wanting something the other is reluctant to give / give up.

Breathing down his neck or cortex

. . . or lose a finger . . .

that the other is reluctant, circumventing

the heart of the matter. In Act Scene we read a soliloquy.
Tell me how we can tell whether Hamlet is mad
and in what sense: crazy or biting

                                    courtiers. We
a game piece. And through the ear
are lines written in keeping with the situation; you have
a mind to assist Stoppard in augmenting the dialogue
spoken by Ros and Guil and if you are to be hired
you will have written in kind, starting with
We are to find out what afflicts Hamlet.

END

Vamp ("Avant-pied")

Why should a man,
in this age of anesthesiology,
seek relief
in the bark of the toothache tree?
Yet, [. . .]

between America's epigraph and epitaph;
yet,
MELVIN B. TOLSON

Of wants that lay in ought's

choking on the index

indeterminate

ancient pain.

Why subsonic sounds you hear of learned pain and obligation

do indict

an untenable posit, position: backspace

practices

pronounced the betwixt and between.

In laughter you acquit

the betwixt divided

by half and half helped into the indecent
parentheses brooding on

reasoning, resonance—too much reverb
lay in the epilogue

granted, a summoning beyond
exodus:

simulcast go forth and between.
And half-cough decibels untenable

prologue, profane morph
you do brood.

Hands tied
to book, some designations anonymous, and yet. . . .

Parentheses subsonic
self-correcting tape. . . .

And the index that contravenes title and thesis
congress of papery

furor I read first to oblige the most inscribed
script

in authorities who are profusely
off-screen

by half reading
scripturally wealthy ancient pain

through aggravated indexes whose authority writes
the author's book

whereas
ascending gainsay

is op cit.
ocean front.

Here and now sacrament
a culture of

the sun
very much in the contemporary style:

are you? "Make conspicuous, evident" of heresy
to be reasonable

with antihistamine extruded from a leaf
the modern chemist

in commencement, inclined to a very limited, in number
relatively little
since rebellion is clearly illegitimate to the existing

amphitheater from dawn's shouting white:
rubric, speak to me!

Not too transgressed
is this Mylar

leaf-turning eventful type so that
(in reverse) no longer intelligible

mendicant
but legible as such

throughout the transistor dust in supposing that
as spouse to the amp seemingly discursive is she likewise

opaque.

Tireless frequenting
a culture of

expenditure hitherto hands tied
to archive, marginalia expiring in the conjecture hastened the

before and after
from dark to dust and dawn to drawn-out indebtedness:

to where?
The poet likes to start from untenable moonlight, the photocopier
in moonlight.

Although you answer the question I asked but not the one I meant
let me take another facsimile

of the sun's
formidable page

and dragged impenetrable

authorship of which may be indexes: mostly prior
names, most cited are not spectacular

corridors, and the sloping ground

devolves

Mylar that takes a bend and fold but does not

find a solution, finds an antidote:

to the lexical comes the graphical

intellect the other said, wrote, and retaliated.

First

antagonism

of graphical and lexical registers as is the transparency yclept

interference of verbal moments swerving through the long exposure

to diaspora and the sloping ground

among nations

you do indict.

Onto staves drawn out legible an odyssey freely ad hoc

not aleatory, the other writhed and wrote

upheaval from which documents and entities were to elapse

from the backspace

diametrically opposite: full stop ran the labyrinth

as the match smoke bespeaks.

Griot Riot

Laying oil over or oil / egg emulsion over dry pigment, a companion
to vision
proprius, or what is one's own, interpellation
to win the book of songs, during, and pin all probability on it
We also address the question: why do cultural movements need performative
stances in manifestos?
Supplement or substrate sub stance subject to will whatsoever
near the surface is a slat brought by the Carpathian Basin's
nonchronological pronouncements
with the advent of agriculture and its attendant technologies by
which the human extends
his hand, et cetera,
I am thinking of a word that rhymes with "nurture"
the arms have worn away; worn away are the armaments against
"an addendum of notes."

You left your umbrella here. Worn away are the armaments:
some speak through aphorism, others harangue; still others enlist reasoning
arguments
wanting the hearer to do something. The tracking number is

a name. Salt, silver, close to the surface

that brought about excavating a decidedly chronological thesis

in glass jars. The loss to your person, what is one's own

coin of the missing dynastic imperative. Please pass the salt, silver

to change the current state of affairs by summoning the ochre.

A bias to sediment and letting it settle: a companion to jars.

In flyswatter negativity of the missing dynastic imperatives

it behooved her

to change the current by summoning the brow

prow for a world that ought to be but that does not yet know

its crazy notes.

The directive for vectors: Which? That? He asked. The bias started

This bias started in 1800, when William Wordsworth composed

"Preface to the Lyrical Ballads."

Gift Idea: frame. The lunatic, then *the very discursive model*

of the lunatic.

Painted surfaces exhortive or prophetic—where did I read this?

Technique,

a companion to vision, wishing to know the transmitters *Attic wit*

and nerve, is that.

Transdanubian communities procured their salt along the routes

mentioned above.

As Technique / As Device /

This maxim
> *This phrase*

High school
> *Lycée student*

Parrot
> *Mouths*

The starting point
> *Point of departure*

Erudite
> *Academic*

Beginning to put together
> *His first stab*

Some kind of systematic
> *At formulating*

This maxim or harpoon
> This phrase and thread

For school and Power On

    Lycée by inches

        A twenty-minute nap and comb

Nap and comb parrot

    How to use

        Mouths

A beginning sound read

    Sounding out the letters

        And what a stylus is

Look Left taking a stab

    Beginning to put together

        His first stab

To apply a maxim

    To swallow said

Saying his first stab

    Mouthing the said brush

Rush hour, poetic and practical

    Turbulence, how to use

The signs the metal squawking
    Self-taught

The parrot begins to put together
    His first stab
        And another thing.

And another thing
    Was combing the topic sentence:

Look Left: School Crossing
    To / from the lycée or fabula

Contribute a crease. Who am I from the village of
    Unbound pages and regime change?

From the start the age of
    Embarkation

Erudition, its Ashanti weights
    The academy as paperweight

The child is beginning to put together the "e" in reverse Watching
the squirrels is
    His first stab, her assay at formulating the parrot.

Now a different example. The child

    A second example. Several men

. . . speech in oneself. And public space or power surge FOR THE
COLLECTIVE WORLD ELECTRIFIED

    Please identity any preexisting conditions (or electrical
    storms) outages to shore

    Embarkation caught the age of reason and thence more lengths

        Art is a way of experiencing the artfulness of an object; the
        object itself is not important.

            Art is a means of experiencing the process of creativity.
            The artifact itself is quite unimportant.

From the village of five fingers

    And percentage on the obverse OF ALL

To assay (or take stabs against) speech

    To begin to put together his first error

        The fact that Japanese poetry has sounds not found
        in conversational Japanese was hardly the first factual
        indication of the differences between poetic and
        everyday language.

The discovery that there are sounds in the Japanese
poetic language that have no parallels in everyday
Japanese was perhaps the first factual indication
that these two languages, that is, the poetic and the
practical, do not coincide.

Erudite spying
    Wary academic

Drops package. "Typical."
    Stands awkwardly "Crumpled hat."

Looking nonstop
devise notation for the ambient sounds
and transcribe unbound pages from the age of reason

    steam from advent of helplessness, used a leaf to let live
to do / not to do
      steam irons arias in
the mouth, the mouth acquiring thunder from touch
    and public space

Look left five minutes
and locate musique concrète
devised for a surfeit of how-not-to-nap
    mouth acquiring steam from the fingers

to do / not to do

        such as questionnaires might well issue.

Find your Times Square and close your eyes to devise a surfeit of
    auditory welts

       Embark on cheap notebook to write only what you hear

. . . the blinds

      Familiar blind spots, theory of

Trial and error intuitive fast processing of unlikeliness

      Back from the end beginning with the germ key term field

Some kind of systemic circuitry

      At formulating circuitous

          Purge

Recursive work is innovative at least to the bass viol

      Strike, stalk the note, implement

Nonpareil blade

     Leaf to push duckling

Erudite spying excites the author of rival discontent

      Academic, you are to bother heeding regime change—

This figure of speech is a poetic trope. (In the first example, "butterfingers" is metonymic; in the second, metaphoric—but this is not what I want to stress.)

> *The image is a poetic trope. (In one case the word* hat *serves as a metonymy, while in the other example we're dealing with a metaphor. And yet I'm really concerned here with something else.)*

At the syntax

Let's have a show of hands

Part II.

Expulsion: A Walking Tour

It cause to walk—conjecture, and yes: translation

I

Walks remain

Walks and their remains

Walks remain the remedial quality

      of lifetimes.

The deadline for the verb was fast approaching.

Cause and conjecture are not one

although they perform together

and walk together.

Expulsion from habitus: all that we have not

walked.

Oh yes he walked off the stage—

as a remark, a stride, a strobe.

He gave conjecture a run for its money when *he walked off the stage*.

Escaping this saucer incongruously

      is

        "cause to walk."

Careful, watch where you're walking.

At that moment they all became naturalists
on a vulnerable walk. A man appeared
To possess an outlook, to have the same experience
as his walking stick.

The spur to walk
implemented
the curvature of *the the.*

"We've a major friction problem here."
"Yes, but" is not a stretch for the practical walk.

WALK / DON'T WALK automated

Walking deregulated the bodies
for the entire gamut of lightning strikes,
tugs. With ballet.

Or concede the following vignette [   ]:
at that moment we all became Otto's story

whose conjecture runs toward thugs deferred
yet correlated to fate;
Stanley's walks self-avoiding.

2

Fast falls the eventide breakthrough.
Walking a few hours protects brain structure.

He walked to the bakery to see her smile
                    after a lost original
at the peripheries of goad.
He conjectured.

Is he serious? *Differing in nature*
out of which ironic walks are

Conjecture is a prolific writer.
"Yes" adapts effortlessly
to elliptical walks.
A leaf in traffic catches a superlative.

The walk cannot be said
to have a vanishing point,
preoccupied as it is with . . .
Translation? Yes.

Not meant for the insolvent
multitudes
and muse he would wake in no-nonsense demolition or another take

of mustard

he gave conjecture a run for its money when *he walked off the stage.*

He goes daily from here to there.

The cause is bread.

She is from there, and he

attains to a walk like a practice of saying.

Endangered walks

Came now to the more open air, conjecture

in twilight's striped vest and stockings:

How to Stroll: A Primer

prolific of 1790, as yes is accomplished

at precipice best yet at Lo!

Stalking through

rapture, the volcano scratched status quo

from our walks. The closer the smoke

the closer I to it.

        Although it choke watercolor, fire

I say: you poison unintentionally.

He flung his arms around a lost cause.

Less possible was the sentence

About You.

Walk for the Cure
receiving an infusion of revolving door's roaring
sunlight: sand in our manifestos
as we upon the ground

Support the Cause

fingering the curvature of *the the*
hear the search for the
blackbird. And it organizes
the spur to walk

Know-how is taking many liberties,
the geneticist whispered.
The American whispered louder.

Two years passed.
A pedestrian happened.
Assisting a literal walk,
he does things.

Another does things with iotas
causes, clouds drawn back:

What do you do? I walk, exclaimed the poet,

And you? His—this, an apprehension and an etiquette. The geneticist

concluded: *my search involves the greatest difference that matters to the
smallest divergence.*

Folding Cythera

I
Whereabouts

would swear by
the etiquette of *the flowers were.*

Now boarding a waiting area

to entitle a swath of
complexion traipsing across the fair debris

that might have had scenographic rebus we shall have thought
    cemented
prospective sympathy rather than retrospective likeness

thought fair vinegar
and encounters with Ursula Oppens at the piano

in wherewithal
exerting a glance up and damp with linen deferred to be read

as sculpture in its own right
performed on the

cavity.

Then again with Ursula Oppens at the piano
sentences will have thought plentifully
about overtaking prospective advances to avert accommodation
                    "What's the matter?"
a companion to warding off conclusive tragedies
and likeness wherein one couple assumed to commence to pause—

at this point the text breaks off.

Whatsoever

now boarding a waiting area such that
atmospheric perspective at arms' length is not so

intrusive as to interfere with the matter
of conjugating the ground upon which to place bodies

as objects mindful of axonometric positions in the minuet.

At this point he breaks into a rivulet
capable of raising its armpit to a condition of alliterative waiting areas.

Retreats and advances stand oriented to each other's hour before dawn.

Let me restate that

averting a tragedy are beings are in favor of awry

trespass across the unlikable metrics thereupon face off and
    accelerating debris
for the throw of the spinet

and there are beings not going
                              "What's bothering you?"
will have thought plentifully

of embarkation away from whereabouts
whose sense data participate in it and how does he sustain her.

Here linen performs a fair swath of sentences
for the cavity now receiving an eventful assist from he who would
    get her to her feet—
is that Paul on the harpsichord.

Appearances seem true
in an escort on his own for the eventful throw of the initiative

discernibly
of trespass and its prerogatives in a wherewithal

attaining to obscure uses
damp within an encampment of fugitives.

The etiquette of *the flowers were.*

2
Taking leave of excerpted bodies:

Folding Cythera

fro or from to and for
whereabouts
now boarding a waiting area

to entitle a swath of
complexion suggests capillaries

that might have had flowers cemented

It is a tempest
undergoing emphasis in subconscious crease

his or her can never get can almost reach might have still
to reach have already *recapitulary*

memories to encounter undergrowth
and others' serrated edges suggestive of motives

To prospective sympathy
this is a tempest voucher

the monthly electrostatic postulate amid
entities gathering up reluctant clothes

and other's serrated edges suggestive of motives
that can never get can almost reach might have

still to reach have already *recapitulary* his or her
skid to entitle a swath of

arm's length.

Segue to skin and its prerogatives.

Atmospheric perspective creeps up in the best-case scenario as
    sounds decay

to afterthought for the eventful conjugal rhetoric performed on

the figure clear and distinct likely but not likable.

                        "Don't mention it,"

scraped against the rim.

                A bowl of

sentences folding discursive wherewithal era in her within earshot
    of he who

shall have scarcely thought to assuage the preexisting deposits

of likeness.

              Stepping forward, head turned back

                                likeness

shall have scarcely thought to assuage the preexisting stencil

performed on the figure

a palm on her whereabouts

                  "What's the matter?"

ironing the other leafage

With open window to begin to fathom greenish blue chill
companion to embarkation

in drastic posits, I am chimera clime childlike chiffon
to do today.

His askance operates a sigh

and for removing grease fremitus felt by placing
speech

on the part of a body via soft white granular variable
cycle to abet cylindrical lyric like

signs that lay a counterclockwise cygnet cyclone
from 1765, they were

ironing the harpsichord and piano together how to
how to do today conjugal infrastructure

in which becoming Paul

does embolden the dear cohort
speech of such an indictment

interspersed.

Ursula,

       face to face, personally.

Sayings

This morning I saw a pretty street whose name is gone.
GUILLAUME APOLLINAIRE / SAMUEL BECKETT

This morning I saw a pretty street whose name I have forgotten.
GUILLAUME APOLLINAIRE / RON PADGETT

I

. . . whose zealous hassle is inconclusive

. . . whose signage is seriously defective.

This morning I saw pretty footage of morning

Is morning: raw footage

Morning saw a pretty espionage

With a pretty questionnaire waving back

Morning saw a prettily shattered glass colorize expletives

Across a spreadsheet.   Whose name is it?

Across a spreadsheet of naval engagement,

I saw an insipid street feel seaworthy.

A flotilla, breathing *like leaves, like sand*

Like leaves are these familiar banners

To some extent expropriating a point whose matter is inadvertent
As I am in words and letters.

As for the plants, she said, "They tolerate my neglect."
The foliage is laughing it off.

. . . whose plumage is a riot with a short beak
. . . whose feather duster wants a fracas.

As I am in words and letters
Parenthetical and fabricated,

This morning saw a picturesque page layout
Pretty as a picture, resembling dawn's early light.

2

This morning saw a pretty street cease to be
The morning saw cease and desist prettily

a dead end whose pretty companion *is felt as an unseen immensity*
This morning's detour whose pretty companion I have not yet seen

. . . whose name is of *a purely allegorical figure*
. . . whose name hastens your face value

Prettily evangelical is this morning's infusion
Prettily sent gospel and wake-up call: The Time Is

Departed. No longer extant, its brightness that much greater
Escaped. Forget about it, frivolous outskirts of the greater area

Street or its fugitive, insistent experiment in waiting
or its immediately anticipated waiting room

. . . whose name? *Replacing the mirage of imagination*
With the mirage of memory, namely

His favorite passage. It was a passing to a causeway
His favorite spot. It was a deportation on the way

To extinction, in brilliant cries flashing on
Standstill, in seasonal calls withdrawn

Unmentionable deportation corrupts a great strength
Banished is the experimental spirit

Trod nomenclature beyond melancholy
Down at the heels—I can't think of the word for it

3

. . . this morning whose name he cannot properly forget

. . . the limbo therefore. This a.m. whose name meant nothing

To an aftermath. This caution, not the same shadow

The stoplight is gone, the flirtatious street is going away.

This morning I saw a pretty egress in a predicament, without souvenirs,

This morning a pretty text in vernacular evasions

Bled identities through the rescue effort whose world is cruelly

Emeritus. A mispronounced street caresses you

Like water in the pipes

Small stream

Of a limbo you squint to read

Understudy for waiting

Where is the hotel? Thank you. A fissure less prodigious

With a subtitle you ought not to miss.

I am thinking of a word, with the suggestion that it never existed

Deceitful street

. . . whose name is extinct

. . .whose name is forgetful

Unbound. Boundless, then. Woe

received word. Stop. As perfected, Go

has a certain gorge. Smiling yielded to broad deletion where our
    favorite cut was

once upon fervent going ovoid. So go the smooth and round

scenarios for the amnesiac.

So go the pretty aliases.

4

That—all gone. Out of ago. Once upon

a time, scaled to going unbegotten

A certain smile vacated the street map and faded enough

The perfectly adequate street tasted mystery the strange goes out
    out of

Wilted signage embraced no plenty discernible to the eye

Loading a street sign: only its banality goes comprehensibly

Unseen symmetry consumes the pretty street notwithstanding harm
    so gorgeous
A dialect unscathed strives to be foxfire and so forth

Wonderful plummeting afterglow you can never find again
Miscued pewter altitude amid steel nil none and / or all

Collapse to vaporize a chasm whose coursing
Dilapidation yet virgin are the unscented

Altitudes themselves engineering off the grid
Depth charges to another I can picture it

Distracted six of one scopic
Even odds diverting a watt

More dashed than thou troubadour
And a solo follows nature's broad hour

To handmade exasperation pulling strings escalating predicates
You so distant escort with the thread in schismatic

Him and her songs of experience
To each other's majestic nausea of lost time

The corporeal slice of
Lo and Behold.

An Ordinary Evening Plus or Minus

Because life is short   improvisatory   requiring grooves: handed a random page of itself
sounds the sticks playing across the drums in shades of   idiom   in cadences and starts
technique not so gone from his memory   idiom derived from ear and formula   addresses
set in marching band "where we learned to play 'cadences.'" Genetic   emulsion of brushes
eddies derived from ear's internal workings gain acquire a small fortune in overture   to
catch strength from the nondeclarative installment   by heart from the same issue, and so
much   *we must remember to keep asking it the same question*   followed by all the rest   the
lion's share.

Until the repeated question and the same silence become answer

In words broken open and pressed to the mouth

And the last silence reveal the lining

in platitude under the regime of sentiment slips through a kind of crepuscule or twilight of
affect wherein the secular world finds a piety ("Fast falls the eventide") by enlisting abuse
gathering to itself rustic spirituality gleaned from administrative dreams *faux bois* that
author   a handful of pathos self-taught   *In words broken open*   guileless lexicon
advancing   *Hasn't the sky?* for one. You learn those things. *The change is not complete*
Wrenched half sentences in the same way   the same question initials   being vastly mortal
grammatical indecently so   the word for what's another word for   please leave word
crepuscule   twilight dusk   saying axiom   saw   maxim   apothegm

The new morals have altered the original data

Which have again outstripped the message deduced from them.

The phenomena have not changed

But a new way of being seen convinces them they have.

From irritability to iteration. Maxim hath suffered reversals. Persons have exited and in their
place third-person plural agency dispenses statements from social science or its simulacrum
to prove—or refute—this script. This script imparts *poncif* to lived octaves   a message apart

the same firm friend   for what was fair weather sentence   will swerve to avoid   strengths
cadenced from side to side   like oxen   probably   as all but one   that are also, somehow.

Yet so blind are we to the true nature of reality at any / given moment that the chaos—
bathed it is true in the iri- / descent hues of the rainbow and clothed in an endless con- /
fusion of fair and variegated forms which did their best to stifle any burgeoning notions of the
formlessness of the / whole, the muddle really as ugly as sin, which at every mo- / ment
shone through the colored masses, bringing a telltale / finger squarely down on the addition
line, beneath which / these self-important and self-convoluted shapes added disconcertingly
up to zero—this chaos began to seem like the / normal way of being, so that sometime later
even very / sensitive and perceptive souls had been taken in: it was for / them life's rolling
river, with its calm eddies and shallows as well as its more swiftly moving parts and ahead of
these / the rapids, with an awful roar somewhere in the distance and marching bands'
salvos confounding those chords played on church organs which may still be heard joining
together in the vernacular through the parody of a homegrown sermon—this species of
Americana put to the test also in the mouth of Paterson whose happenings on sundry
Sundays in the park do occur frequently enough to be part of the public record awash with
din; *and yet, or so it seemed to these more sensible than aver- / age folk, a certain amount of*
hardship has to be accepted / if we want the river-journey to continue life cannot be a /
series of totally pleasant events, and we must accept the / bad if we also wish the good;
indeed a certain amount of / evil is necessary to set it in the proper relief: how could we /
know the good without the experience of the opposite? / And so these souls took over and
dictated to the obscurer / masses that follow in the wake of the discoverers. The way / was
picturesque and even came to seem carefully thought / out   the garden   the garden path
whose platitudes   instruct the family to pace itself   with respect to the way   how and where
crepuscule   saying   a brook you thought   had anticipated rivers and mountains   name
twenty   children's games   destinations the vacuous category not   cutting the mustard   up
to snuff   does not compute   the word   a handful of appearances   loosely federated
appurtenances may be apt to suggest it accessories   trappings   appendages
accoutrements   equipment   paraphernalia impedimenta   bits and pieces   things

And so these souls   Doric   Corinthian   once thought   Why not *The Death of Marat?*

Because   polis and change   brain   habit through foliage with vastly more courtesy to

neurons   in chosen field fold folding bonds among posits   allies alleys allay   always

articulate with respect to the concept and unambivalent breathing

In addition to these twin notions of growth, two kinds of happiness are possible: the frontal

and the latent populate the wire racks found in some   waiting   synapses writing more fluent

than speaking   summarize paragraph in a sentence   silvering *tain* stations which negotiate

a   conversation excavation exhortation from then on   it was   having been revealed the

word for "deterrent"? Antidote   lobes   cameo parietal frameworks changing words into

thoughts   *noble simplicity and quiet grandeur,* for one   self-help guides to pauses or

metacommentary   airports to elevate populist horizons   the airport   lounges once thought

to negotiate home with away through something like willpower have arrived at memoranda:

there is here diminished. The mindset of yes, but. Something like misshapen protein occurs

in the happiness which intrigues and in the forced nonpareil is okay. Ungainly Dos and

Don'ts   hence poetic furtherance. If the text aspires to a poetics it is through code-switching

complicated in a rhetorical pratfall from which pathos issues. He has been studying his

inspirational literature assiduously, as the pamphlets' analytical formatting of a concept

betrays   pharmacies and train stations proliferates   airport lounges with impairment and

recovery: where to begin? Having just considered life as career and passed on to life as

ritual, the poet further entertains the role of the writer of instruction manuals through which

his poetics had had its formative moment, to once again revisit a favorite cultural dystopia:

the practical somewhere.

To be or not to be   agape through inelegant chromaticism   may shape ANTIQUES Always

modern fakes et cetera in this poetics   three kinds of   twinned   dialectical interfacing for

blindness and insight   the selvage.

How the sentence treats such disorders with infinite patience   finite categories befall to heal

substance. It came to pass   currently a lifetime of approach-avoidance camouflage   might

get therapeutic *Life is short, and Art long; the crisis fleeting; experience perilous, and*
decision difficult.

Right now it is important to slip / as quickly as possible into the Gordian contours of the /
dank, barren morass (or so it seems at present) without ut- / tering so much as a syllable. . . .
Mortal twill   Cut the nonsense for the man who has everything, to bring decision with it;
attached is raveling sense such that each phrase undoes or undercuts the assertion just
previous through contrarily indicated postures and qualifying statements meant to shore up
a confidence toward life. The upshot: a linguistic gargoyle of false equivalences,
insupportable as decadence, does constitute a negative resolve even as it would abuse not
void a sea of trouble. Of burial and its avatars are the deliberately "divisive and incoherent"
desires *to live in that labyrinth that / seems to be directing your steps but in reality it is you*
who / are creating its pattern, embarked on a new, fantastically / difficult tactic whose
success is nonetheless guaranteed. You know this. Thinking positively comes arbitrarily to
conclude that which it does assert but not prove. Relay zeal in raveling   mainstay the realm
"unleashing your potential" filters through "seminars"   drops typhoons through a sieve
Mind your Business minted   supposing the entire enterprise   reprise healing and parlor   as
hydrangea   and coil beyond

Yours Truly, for one   voicing for advice indemnity   possible damage loss or injury   into
thought   distinguish Realism from Naturalism   to chisel populist from bituminous   what is
an author   an awl   employ the word   name ten implements for exciting neurons   in chosen
maze posit   meanders   disputing nicely   allies always   articulate with respect to *allées* for
the design principle interdiscursive to pause for metacommentary such that it explores
weeds in late modernity   allay   abyss inwardness

Leverage individual *Today your wanderings have come full circle. Having / begun by*
rejecting the idea of oneness in favor of a plural- / ity of experiences. . . . The figure
"full circle" is the dead metaphor to be deployed at cortex withdrawal to draw to a
conclusion that which has been throughout the book-length drift and passive song to
will. Thus

sleep and watchfulness

which you wish. *All right. The problem is that there is no new problem. It / must awaken from the sleep of being part of some other, / old problem and by that time its new problematical exist- / ence will have already begun, carrying it forward into situ- / ations with which it cannot cope, since no one recognizes it and it / does not even recognize itself yet, or know what it is.* That one just mentioned. Fresh camouflage selective provinciality fluctuating disinterment bent "—used as the subject of a verb that describes a condition or occurrence. —used in the place of a noun, phrase, or clause that usually" girds abrupt ultimatum from queasiness chronic in the text visited upon him.

What is it for you then, the insistent now that baffles / and surrounds you in its loose-knit embrace that always / seems to be falling away and yet remains behind, stub- / bornly drawing you, the unwilling spectator who had / thought to stop only just for a moment, into the sphere of / its sudden and solemnly vast activities, on a new / scale as it were, that you have neither the time nor the / wish to unravel? It always presented itself as the turning / point, the bridge leading from prudence to "a timorous capacity," in Wordsworth's phrase. . . . "The Figure in the Carpet" wherein lack of referent in close rereading and yet athletic relay makes common cause with non sequitur: there were   numbers   stunning the harried mind I am thinking of a number of streaks   thinking a word I am thinking of a word for "something that cuts" number twelve satisfying this function. Untrouble life. Sustain something that ferments happiness without our looking; accept gifts of festal joy that attends coiling rivers and mountains. Define "fermentation." Symptom above all converting time to opportunity "Precept: a rule for living; a command or principle for life. Proverb: a short pithy saying in general use, stating a general truth or piece of"   poverty   causative   on the switch cognitive   if true, we could   half-surging   toxicity   yet   over the crest of an expedition from which there is no escape   express expedient entity in experimental Mylar that takes a crease intelligibly   Mylar that takes a crease and my decision intelligibly   upon the ground my decision to further a modern fold unspoken and so put it to admiring architects of whom I asked whether there had been or could be a reason to decline to build, the eventfulness being chora at or upon the surface of the ground occurring—but that was coincidental. To return is no simple story: to turn a leaf of Mylar is to encounter interference from graphic overlay upon lexical intention   to return fruition here. Multiply. Coincidentally, to turn a leaf of Mylar is to encounter interference from lexical overlay upon graphical intention   to return pixelated back and forth   yet opaque pages create a studio. In earth something valid in earth something valid   and something begun in provident narratives   in providential concepts that constitute a priori sayings   sayings in contretemps to maneuver influence at the seems that went nowhere. Although architect and philosopher could neither exit nor further the fault lines to write without some borrowed impressiveness, another's spur edged out   spurt   esprit to write   land yet would soon be sod   three kinds of sound   entity expiry date did write: that's not an essay but a bridge   a walkway speculating fragrantly above the lawn's postulated play   name twelve ball games   define "idyll"   that's not an easy excursus   of yellow   enviable digression so too the dreamwork   the dream much admired the language it taught the patient to write himself   impatient nest venting basket   brise-soleil screen straining   wetlands, actually   architecture inclined to strain a sieve through which antimonumentality endemic awakenings ebbed the same irony ever suspended in flesh to be read   and yet again as sea surface besotted with clouds the imitations sloshing camouflage efflux   *emptiness distributed ventilated situations* sated plenitude within hail of fade. To have heard is to have tone clusters sour on the pulse and lain upon irritability's dying as tidal foam sometimes. He declines to build.

There were new people watching and waiting, conjugating in this / way the distance and emptiness,   overture and march   together as one recedes the other advancing advises not without   dénouement that is carpet within the figure   inflammation   distributing the scuffed   motif   insouciant calligraphic iteration taut enough to take a swipe yet in itself indifferent. Décor which may be defined as wishful thinking has correlated the diffusion of good taste to idiolect as if   as if these slats   as if to say that this may be his substance kept at bay   modernity deflated to a placebo and so adhering to an air of elementary blunders. He has much Expulsion: A walking tour. Poetics: text of the lyric: how long can it build a force field of apathy? Lassitude and its avatars intricate scarcity wove   a waywardness that entices others to "identify" or be induced to *transforming the scarcely / noticeable bleakness into something both intimate and / noble.*

*I thought that if I could put it all down that would be / one way. And next the thought came to
me that to leave / all out would be another, and truer, way.*

     Clean-washed sea

             The flowers were.

A statement of poetics. A statement of poetics inherited in the courses of modernist origins
that give the contemporary poet his discourse, and his fatigue. The weight of cultural
memory ("I've read all the books") a tincture of which infuses the quandary
of which way to take

        Not the / truth, perhaps, but—yourself. It is you who made this,

        a walk so symbolist.

*A segment, more, of reality. This must be / remembered too, it is even important, but will
the / parody to establish norm within a proverbial sense* be seen even as thought to protect
the noncommittal ordinary evening?

*The performance has ended, the audience streamed out; the applause still echoed in the
empty hall. But the idea of the spectacle as something to be acted out / and absorbed still
hung in the air long after* forms gather at the river

or with

     as having a

Aesthetic Education

of the violent word MIR *painted green.*
OXOTA, LYN HEJINIAN

of the violent word MIR *painted green*

Guided by writers
we read the land and landscape as they do. Other writings of a
theoretical nature, such as . . .

the riddle

. . . and what is that to natural land, landscape—or property? In dire
poverty yet with a poetics not so dire the age acquires

an anecdote

each character to reflect the vogue for improving grounds as
would be practiced through landscape, the vogue for grounds,
improvement in the leaping fence

of the rapid housing block

in transit: now all the world a startling whereabouts guided by
writers, a startling wherewithal

of the violent word PEACE

The walking tour became very popular, even extending beyond
   the pale and elsewhere bequest. Of what significance for
   Romantic literature is the walking tour? The walking tour
   became. What were

the riddles.

Gardens and parks, fens and wilderness, pursuant to pacifying
   domesticated passage from shady to shadowy park

in housing blocks

to park Xanadu, imagine wilderness from without, the preserve of
   several thousand shadows flourishing amid her faces, her flavors,
   and imagine the pleasure terraced without the preserve of paradise.

From the terrace the young people wandered away through the
   meander, they liked losing their statistics to the

riddle whose foliage had been thinned to

the noisy shade—woods rather than forest, the terms of—wherein
   putting stains out to pasture is relatively less dense to the

riddle whose foliage had been thinned to let in the picturesque
   violent WORLD

of sumptuous fens, febrile wilderness, meadows so noisy yet also
    prevailing upon chocks put under the sensibility within which
    several gardens shoreth loquaciousness in upward terraces to lift
    a better situation from which to view a wordy forest

in a northern housing district

                for whose ageing stains the cityscape
                advocates a perpetual use
    the inscription in memoriam seen past the finishing line where the
        marathon congregated this morning
                    for instance.

To riddle

walks through gardens and parks, fens and wilderness, guided by
    writers Wordsworth, Clare, Coleridge, Austen, Ruskin, and
    others, we read landscape as they do land scaled to an estimate

transposed to the Alps

of syllables

reflected vocationally onto MIR *painted green.*

Anecdotal evidence of meer green cumbersome words, several
    thoughts, several thousand worries, syllables at once numerous,
    several thousand counterarguments

to pierce with holes throughout a sieve

to riddle with syllables

Mixed-use and zoning change the complexion of elongated green
    stains. And what must the tour guides say: this was Greenwich
    Village? This is once upon a time? Inverting the fabric of

a vivacious anecdote

the alphabet from the Alps to a terrain scaled to a short tour

of estimates, we try to attain to longevity in moist footings of
    neighborhood from send to receive circa what little remains
    of traceable letters up to and including the greater airshaft and
    sunlight written

between tenements

pied. The green word world wariness worries the vigilant reflection
    level with the course of the vignette. New retail, some in keeping
    with the elegy, the old purpose with locale for some

housing

changes style. That the tour amused itself too with lore easily
tending the embellishments is retelling memory—we are on a
spree of circumstantial incidents, says the bystander. Yes, to the
mismatched stone wrinkle, he

of the housing block

noted, to mirror the discrepant fabric of which he approved, the
urbanist remarked, not necessarily to read the volition the same,
said the heroine sadly. Her guess was now the very tongue of
valley glen chasm gorge ravine

and the MIR

intercepting the history of gardens the genius of place mountain
gloom abounding roman of the rose ten books on architecture
memorabilia and oeconomicus

the victorious epigram

the virtuous horizontality

the vicious epigram

with green stains

the vicarious epigram

the violet staining

approved the stone on which it rested scampered some minutes

photographed the guest shadow as

the event

Surfaces organized their own work not necessarily to read the volition,
    said a storm, noting the pavement wherein lay the wrinkle: our
    tree heaved the blue rider enjoying volition with a new preface.

Surfaces

  will be found to be strictly the language of prose when prose is well written.

Ordinary language
                a poetics worth investigating, but

I am thinking of a word

virulent

integer for plots estates improving grounds to show the seam.
    Theatricals she wore lent the writing desk a comedy of manners
    whereby to entrance the social discourse: epistolary propriety
    had to tease the forces whose motives are patently obvious

anecdotal

main chance leafy comeuppance presenting the complement then
    the demand to be introduced to X, the social contract inverting
    the Ps and Qs written on a vine-leaf and whence the sent vignette

is MIR

war and world. To plot the path of the broad-leafed predicate that
   would estimate culturally discrepant walks by those Roman
   military companions seen in conversation that dawdled abundantly
   as they strolled back and forth speculating rather than

housing

purpose is to appear crazy to the other. Walks must be to some
   purpose, they must not defeat their own death by means of
   campaign's time out, short shrift and *poetic language* [that] *gives
   voice to the fluxes and*

violent riddle violet riddle

of the mind when agitated by the great and simple

green

stairs stares tympanum bells sticks on pavement rim brush
   omnivorous brusque benches water fountains lavatories kiosks
   directories maps plans

resting on nothing
the suspension bridge

in leverage sustaining of the most elevated *technē* not to say labor
must necessarily, *except*

might be demonstrated through innumerable utopia

cupola

word used

word MIR *painted green*

CLEAR GLASS SQUARE LEANING said the protagonist of the sentence;
the urbanist said, "Cupola is a word," and yet to the world said
again WALL, YOU ARE MINE

invariably violent cleft

of awe being no actual direct threat throughout the broad-leaved
predicate, put rhetoric as writ large public negation, to cleave
"The one who owns the world" (it comes from two Russian words:
"vladet"—"to possess" and "mir"—"the world."

of the housing block.

Ask the wall and assert the attic: wayfaring stranger, maintain the
tomb of

the house

Last Whole Earth Catalog catches opening glades / Joins willing wood,
    and varies

the house to move it

to speculate on the rays of late and esteem them as thought in the
    evidential stipple we read; that wall pitted seemingly as the pity
    of light's closer inspection

stain

viols voicing the shadows within which light was the revealed
    common prayer, the bystander was heard to have said and to
    have touched

housing blocks in themselves.

A curiosity: abstract mass may be said to exist in the Suprematist
    models for mass only in the generality extruding *the the* the
    urbanist thought—and an unoccupied *avant-pied* comparable to
    an event said the curator reading his thoughts and dancing away
    to refill his glass

house.

Guess who? Guess what? asked the narrator of senders and receivers, putting his finger on the vignette *That tells the Waters to rise, or fall, / Or helps th' ambitious Hill.* The curator is at it again, said she, turning over a short tour of *the fluxes and*

riddling ribbing

fan vault. Is this being responsible, I asked, to which he responded FAN VAULT PERPENDICUAR STYLE Oh, I said, conjoined. Normal capitals sprang into my head thoughtlessly perhaps yet no less significantly overdetermined. Normal capitals, said he, weighing

the word MIR,

befit the *many-branched student* also. *Not responsible but interesting, you said.* Propagate the shadows of narrative but then compare with prewar cinema, senders hidden in the transversals

riddle

and rendezvous. Riddled with rendezvous and free fall is the city.

Written on a vine leaf:
Crises come of their own accord and need not be induced.
Let us all be strong and help those in need.

from **Of Autobiography**

Of Autobiography

1

She shall never forget
cardiac inkstand + because life is short + on off on of + ENTER

2

On off on of + ENTER the same jury
to be read as much as seen to be causing
arrhythmias within the frame because.

3

Because life is short
decisive black gray white declarative
we must remember to EXIT the parenthesis.

4

Yellow leaves lively
hurricane on off on of
valve.

5

Cardiac inkstand because life is on off on of
before, during and after, hotter
as we use up our utterances.

6

Because life is short although itinerant
we must keep remembering these infusions
of that estate of only as a prompt to issuing
the same gray scale questionnaire
of unremarked questions we are not asking.

7

ENTER palpitating inkstand
because life is a mote.

8

You, excerpted heart—
such on off on of
is and is.

9

I was of a mind to
offer a cause
to an abbreviated life,
a motive
to a hard life,
and a prose
to enter into.

10

We, the entire bronze
cardiovascular life
at the entrance to
ink, the living hemoglobin
involving head, headings, headlines.

11

Farther up the processional route
ENTER no more beyond
yes, but with even odds
that companion to
month of Sundays.

12

Because life—or a different song with a similar beginning
then becoming that companion to on off on of—
is short shrift.

13

At heart a lung would do arterial ink
in deep retirement beating frequently
with beat frequency breach.
He stopped where he was.

Stranded Speech in Walkabout Time

Because life is short, keep remembering
the knowledge of that: those words are ours.
And the fallow deer.

Because life is short

We must keep remembering to ask the same question

Because platitude then non sequitur
warning us not to trust writing
wherein the nonsensical proposition in a rustic photocopy of
    the eternal—
this, a rendering by the author himself
at the syntax of an effluvium wherein sentences recognize subtitles
    as their own species.
A bronze inkstand we have admired more than once
sits upon appointments, information, and inquiries, the cuttings of
    which require a repeat or a repeal.
There is no sentence. On the contrary.
It is not to be: because life then non sequitur warning us not to
    trust writing
this lawn as these deer at the heart
render a bronze inkstand we have admired more than once.

Fray

Unfolded dark

    and whatever may be done in the dark

Shot of interior

moving lights

Ignite dark

  with thought to "solving" that which is unclear in the aftermath

      by magnifying it

through a water glass, eye glasses, under glass

Ignite desk.

  But for the legibly scanned time machine

      do not operate emergency quietus

Because life

felt for eye

  magnifying the flashlight's glassy face-off

      of the mirror where floated the folded eyeglass case.

Ignite desk askance.

Felt glass

  magnifying the wine-dark mirror

Massive dark news

  recurs

unfolding the desk's evening

    Ask the same question this

evening but from another angle.

Interior shot

of moving light

A glass

through which wristwatch is anamorphic with mirror

Felt for eye

Shot of her reading

the because of facing pages

    the because of white paper.

      She asks: does R's screenplay maintain

        that M forfeits X when X moves

          apprehension to anticipation

           in the gaze of the

        statues?

Shot of her reading

she having reached for her tableau.

Voiceover:

Where are you going?

He: 53rd Street

She: 53rd Street, near there.

The because of facing pages

    reflected in the glass

causing you to stand aside the glare.

The water glass felt touched.

Shot of bus stop

Do you suppose
    that M's controlling the plot
        involved his loss of A
            or was irrelevant concerning that?

I come from Morocco
    to assist with the screening
        of Arab experimental film
            to open today.

I am also going there
    or near there but not until tomorrow
        or I shall never go there
            or I should
                or I would love to go there.

Roman Stone

As life is short, repair it in peace—in the aftermath, programming traffic for flow has spoken on the avenue and would start eliminating seconds. You are right, ice is quite impossible. Steam, then? To keep traffic flowing in the aftermath of a flood, continuous movement has given way to synchronized halting. Of shoreline posted, transposed, programmed, with fluid vehicular traffic issuing in signals: silence, then a hum almost masking ionized sirens. Because life is short, we must memorandize ebb. Tide posted around a storm drain. Vapors going for mileage. Solid traffic evaporates. Traffic clings to flash, almost immediately. Stop. Rhetoric is speech, is speech that ingratiates.

You are right. Ice would be out of the question.

Word Made Flesh

Because life is short
cells are programmed to die unless notified not to.

Because life is short
nothing is easier than overtaking the future

the certainties arising only from sluggishness, Mallarmé's
bulging, a specific milieu in tissue where once existed entelechies
sheathing lapsed soggy.

Things fall apart
immature or silly patriot *present only in*

going or going on in italics of bereavement, shrinkage in our read-
ing

our removal from the cell *Tel Quel* or "The division of the assem-
bly"
for attention spans somewhat less.

Now you see it
cellular wreck where sputtered tissue or less work.

To regulate a good duplicate we must remember to issue duplicate
pleats. Et cetera ingesting disintegration—
daughter no respite from self.

Ready or not
death a preservative selected *the degenerative process.*

So too barrage *present to adult but with loss of endocrine* wherewithal
the said adaptor cleaving complex triggers cascade:
we must remember to cherish shrinkage cell wall vacuole

to fall away fall apart
present only in embryonic stage, then bestowed
adult removal.

Here today
flowers attack the touch

that would crave an intercellular agenda
spoken for. The said adaptor
now diminished, the cell settled (a caucus having been to the area).
    We, anew.

Time flies
at tissue

Question: why doubt atrophy's thorough bulging?

Gather ye rosebuds
cell death

Coffee House Press began as a small letterpress operation in 1972 and has grown into an internationally renowned nonprofit publisher of literary fiction, essay, poetry, and other work that doesn't fit neatly into genre categories.

Coffee House is both a publisher and an arts organization. Through our *Books in Action* program and publications, we've become inter-disciplinary collaborators and incubators for new work and audience experiences. Our vision for the future is one where a publisher is a catalyst and connector.

LITERATURE
is not the same thing as
PUBLISHING

Funder Acknowledgments

Coffee House Press is an internationally renowned independent book publisher and arts nonprofit based in Minneapolis, MN; through its literary publications and *Books in Action* program, Coffee House acts as a catalyst and connector—between authors and readers, ideas and resources, creativity and community, inspiration and action.

Coffee House Press books are made possible through the generous support of grants and donations from corporations, state and federal grant programs, family foundations, and the many individuals who believe in the transformational power of literature. This activity is made possible by the voters of Minnesota through a Minnesota State Arts Board Operating Support grant, thanks to the legislative appropriation from the arts and cultural heritage fund, along with a grant from the Wells Fargo Foundation Minnesota. Coffee House also receives major operating support from the Amazon Literary Partnership, the Bush Foundation, the Jerome Foundation, The McKnight Foundation, Target, and the National Endowment for the Arts (NEA). To find out more about how NEA grants impact individuals and communities, visit www.arts.gov.

Coffee House Press receives additional support from the Elmer L. & Eleanor J. Andersen Foundation; the David & Mary Anderson Family Foundation; the Buuck Family Foundation; the Carolyn Foundation; the Dorsey & Whitney Foundation; Dorsey & Whitney LLP; the Knight Foundation; the Rehael Fund of the Minneapolis Foundation; the Matching Grant Program Fund of the Minneapolis Foundation; the Schwab Charitable Fund; Schwegman, Lundberg & Woessner, P.A.; the Scott Family Foundation; the US Bank Foundation; VSA Minnesota for the Metropolitan Regional Arts Council; the Archie D. & Bertha H. Walker Foundation; and the Woessner Freeman Family Foundation in honor of Allan Kornblum.

The Publisher's Circle of Coffee House Press

Publisher's Circle members make significant contributions to Coffee House Press's annual giving campaign. Understanding that a strong financial base is necessary for the press to meet the challenges and opportunities that arise each year, this group plays a crucial part in the success of Coffee House's mission.

Recent Publisher's Circle members include many anonymous donors, Mr. & Mrs. Rand L. Alexander, Suzanne Allen, Patricia A. Beithon, Bill Berkson & Connie Lewallen, the E. Thomas Binger & Rebecca Rand Fund of the Minneapolis Foundation, Robert & Gail Buuck, Claire Casey, Louise Copeland, Jane Dalrymple-Hollo, Ruth Stricker Dayton, Jennifer Kwon Dobbs & Stefan Liess, Mary Ebert & Paul Stembler, Chris Fischbach & Katie Dublinski, Kaywin Feldman & Jim Lutz, Sally French, Jocelyn Hale & Glenn Miller, the Rehael Fund-Roger Hale/Nor Hall of the Minneapolis Foundation, Randy Hartten & Ron Lotz, Jeffrey Hom, Carl & Heidi Horsch, Amy L. Hubbard & Geoffrey J. Kehoe Fund, Kenneth Kahn & Susan Dicker, Stephen & Isabel Keating, Kenneth Koch Literary Estate, Jennifer Komar & Enrique Olivarez, Allan & Cinda Kornblum, Leslie Larson Maheras, Lenfestey Family Foundation, Sarah Lutman & Rob Rudolph, the Carol & Aaron Mack Charitable Fund of the Minneapolis Foundation, George & Olga Mack, Joshua Mack, Gillian McCain, Mary & Malcolm McDermid, Sjur Midness & Briar Andresen, Maureen Millea Smith & Daniel Smith, Peter Nelson & Jennifer Swenson, Marc Porter & James Hennessy, Jeffrey Scherer, Jeffrey Sugerman & Sarah Schultz, Nan G. & Stephen C. Swid, Patricia Tilton, Stu Wilson & Melissa Barker, Warren D. Woessner & Iris C. Freeman, Margaret Wurtele, Joanne Von Blon, and Wayne P. Zink.

For more information about the Publisher's Circle and other ways to support Coffee House Press books, authors, and activities, please visit www.coffeehousepress.org/support or contact us at info@coffeehousepress.org.

MARJORIE WELISH is the author of *The Annotated "Here" and Selected Poems, Word Group, Isle of the Signatories,* and *In the Futurity Lounge / Asylum for Indeterminacy,* all from Coffee House Press. The papers delivered at a conference on her writing and art held at the University of Pennsylvania were published in the book *Of the Diagram: The Work of Marjorie Welish* (Slought Books). In 2009, Granary Books published *Oaths? Questions?,* a collaborative artists' book by Marjorie Welish and James Siena, which was the subject of a special exhibition at Denison Museum in Granville, Ohio; the book is in permanent collections, including that of the Metropolitan Museum of Art. Recent art exhibitions have occurred at Emanuel von Baeyer Cabinet, London, and Ruskin Gallery, Cambridge. *So What So That* came to completion thanks to a John Simon Guggenheim Memorial Foundation Fellowship. Her further honors include the George A. and Eliza Gardner Howard Fellowship from Brown University, the Judith E. Wilson Visiting Fellowship in Poetry at Cambridge University, and two fellowships from the New York Foundation for the Arts. She has held a Senior Fulbright Fellowship, which has taken her to the University of Frankfurt and to the Edinburgh College of Art. She is now Madelon Leventhal Rand Chair of Literature at Brooklyn College.

So What So That was designed by
Bookmobile Design & Publisher Services.
Text is set in Dante MT Pro, a typeface designed
by Giovanni Mardersteig in the mid-1950s.